My Book About The Body

Everybody's body is different! This book uses big, bright photographs and simple text to describe the different parts of the body and how it works. It looks at faces, hair, arms, hands, legs and feet. It also explains how to stay fit and healthy by eating the right food, washing, exercising and resting. The words and pictures have been carefully chosen to develop reading skills and promote interest and discussion.

My Book About

The Body
Clothes
Food
Houses and Homes
Toys
Weather

Editor: Anna Girling
Designer: Loraine Hayes

First published in 1991 by
Wayland (Publishers) Ltd
61 Western Road, Hove
East Sussex BN3 1JD, England

British Library Cataloguing in Publication Data
Jackman, Wayne
My book about the body. – (My book about)
I. Title II. Series
428.4

ISBN 0 7502 0121 5

Typeset by Kalligraphic Design Ltd, Horley, Surrey
Printed and bound by Casterman S.A., Belgium

Words that are **underlined** in the text are explained in the glossary on page 22.

My Book About

The Body

WAYNE JACKMAN

Wayland

Everybody is different. Some people are short and others are tall.

Legs can be long and feet can be small.
What size are you?

People have different coloured skin.

Hair can be many different colours too.
Is your hair long or short?
Is it curly or straight?

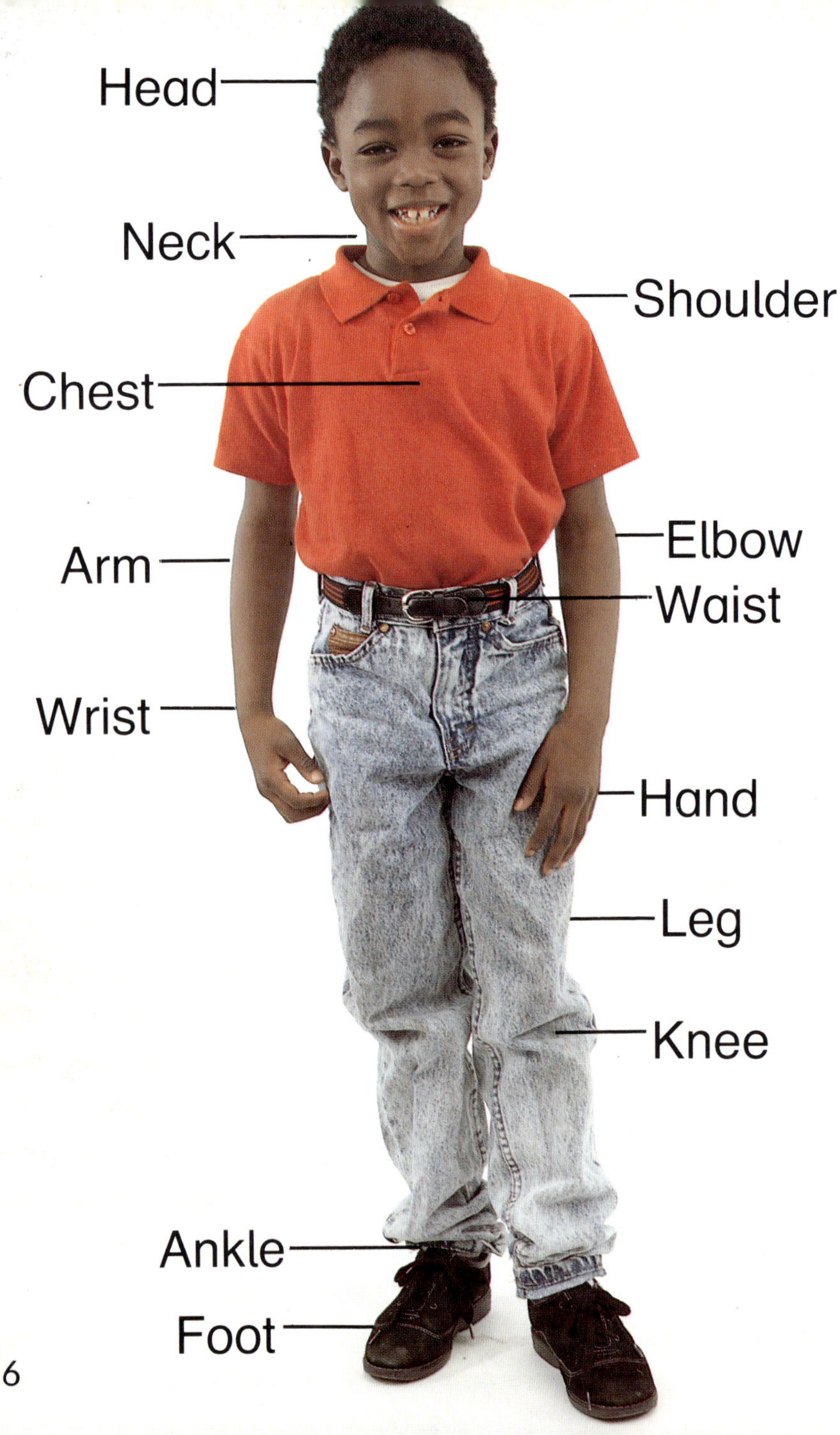

Your body has many parts. The parts all have names. **Do you know where your elbow is?**

Look at the picture. It tells you where everything is.

Faces have lots of parts too.
Point to the parts you know.

Look at the **freckles** on the girls' faces.
Can you count them?

Our arms
can bend at
the elbow.
This boy
is holding
a bat.
He is
bending his
arms to hit
a ball.

Try bending
your arms
up and down.

We can hold things in our hands.
This girl is holding a pencil. She is writing with it.

Which hand do you write with?

Legs are very strong.
They help us to run and jump.
Can you run very fast?

Dancers need
strong legs
and feet.
These girls are
ballet dancing.

**Can you point
your toes
like this?**

Inside your body are lots of **bones**. They are joined together to make a **skeleton**.

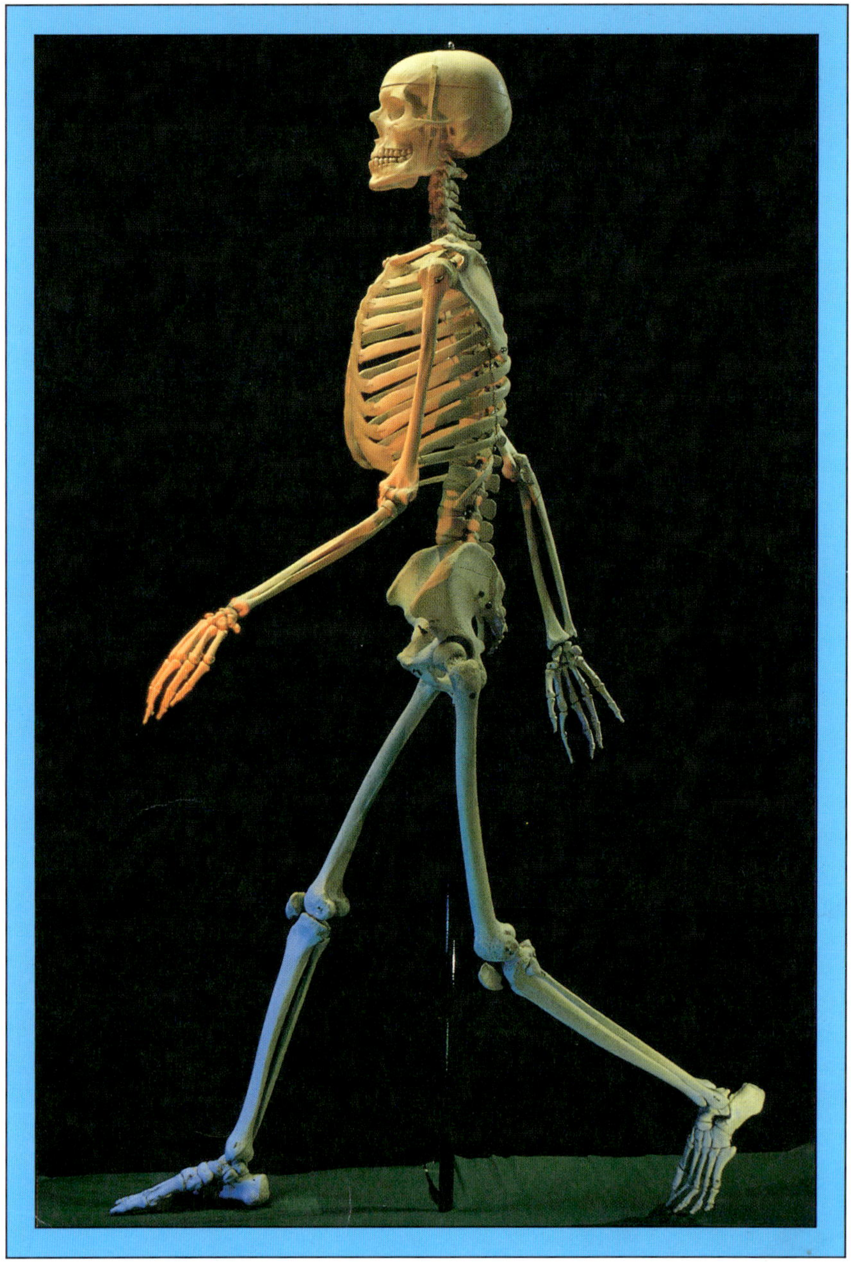

Squeeze your arms and legs. **Can you feel the bones?**

Healthy food is good for your body. It helps your body to grow strong. **Fruit** and **vegetables** are good for you.

Do you eat lots of healthy food?

Everybody needs to **breathe**. We take in air through our noses.

Is this boy breathing in or out?

Our bodies get dirty.
We need to wash every day.

This boy is having a shower.
Does he like his shower?

Playing sport keeps us healthy.
Do you play football?

What sport do you like best?

When our bodies get tired we need to rest.
Sleep is very good for us.

What is this boy holding?

Here are some children riding bicycles. They are wearing **helmets**.

If the children fall off, the helmets will stop them from hurting their heads.

This boy is ill.
He is in **hospital**.

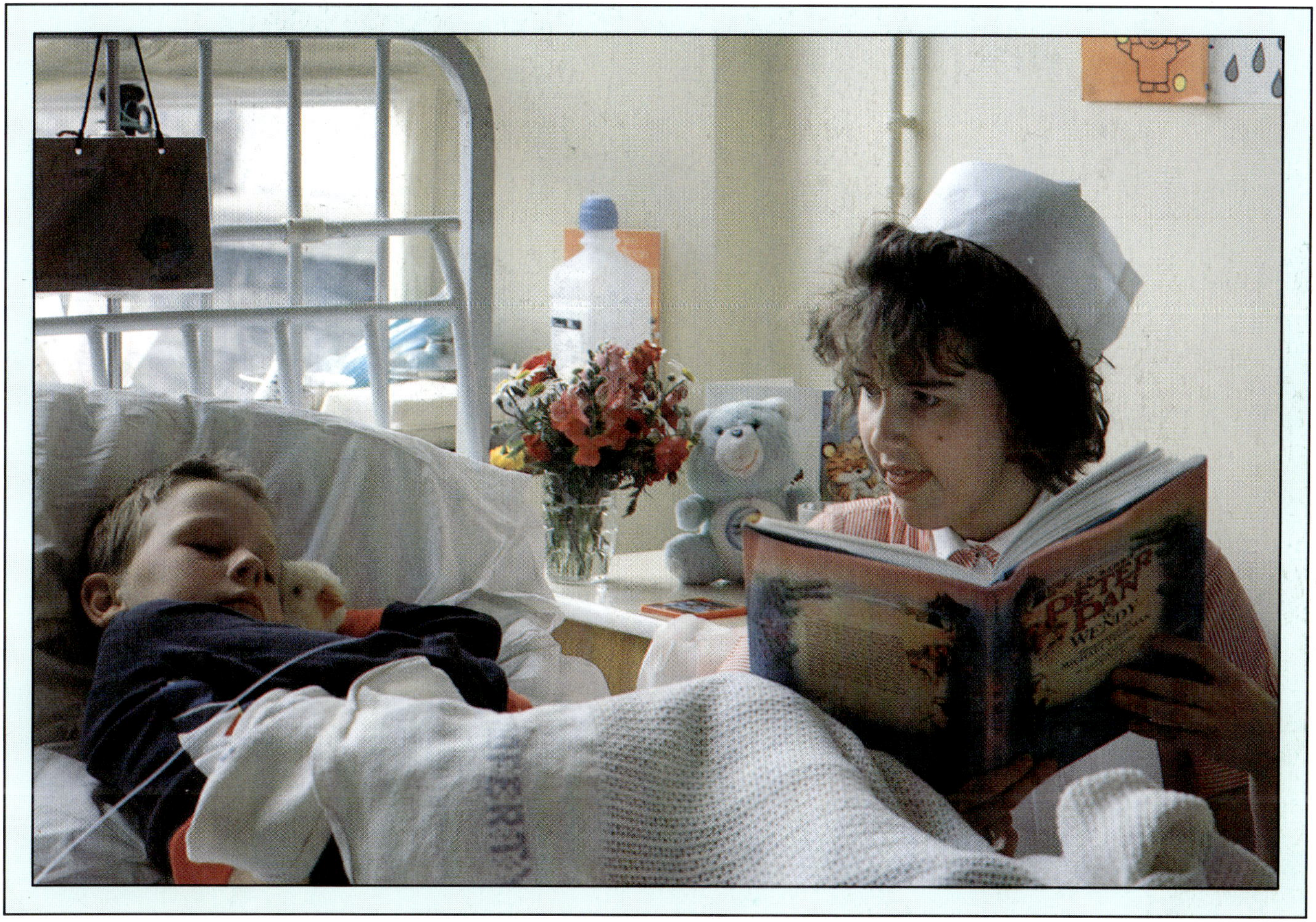

The **nurse** is looking after him.
Soon he will be better.

People grow old.
Our hair turns grey as we grow old.
This boy likes to walk with his grandfather.

Why are they holding sticks?

Here is a whole family.

There are the grandparents, mum and dad and the three children.
Who is the oldest?

Glossary

Ballet dancing A kind of dancing that is very graceful and has special moves and steps.

Bones The hard parts inside your body that join together to make your skeleton.

Breathe To take in air through the nose or mouth and let it out again.

Freckles Small brown spots that some people have on their skin.

Fruit The part of a plant that grows around the seed. It is usually soft and juicy and is good to eat.

Healthy Good for your health. Health means the general state of your body, whether you are well or ill.

Helmets Hard hats that protect the head.

Hospital A place where people are looked after if they are ill or hurt.

Nurse A person whose job is to look after people who are ill or hurt.

Skeleton The framework of bones inside the body of a human or animal.

Vegetables The parts of plants that are eaten as food.

Books to read

Food by Kay Davies and Wendy Oldfield (Wayland, 1991)
Look at Faces by Henry Pluckrose (Franklin Watts, 1987)
Look at Feet by Henry Pluckrose (Franklin Watts, 1987)
Look at Hair by Ruth Thomson (Franklin Watts, 1987)
Look at Hands by Ruth Thomson (Franklin Watts, 1987)
My Body by Ruth Thomson and Beverley Mathias (Franklin Watts, 1988)
Senses by Kay Davies and Wendy Oldfield (Wayland, 1991)
Skeletons and Movement by Kay Davies and Wendy Oldfield (Wayland, 1991)

For older readers:
Body Power by Jenny Vaughan (Cherrytree Books, 1990)
Why Does My Heart Beat? by Dr Philip Whitfield and Dr Ruth Whitfield (Natural History Museum Publications, 1988)

Picture acknowledgements

The publishers would like to thank the following for providing the photographs for this book: Chapel Studios 6, 14; Eye Ubiquitous 8; Eileen Langsley (Supersport Photographs) cover; Science Photo Library 12 (Manfred Kage); Tony Stone Worldwide 5 (Chris Harvey), 10 (Chris Harvey), 11 (John Garrett), 16; Timothy Woodcock 4, 9, 15; Zefa 7, 13 (Parker), 17, 18 (Tatiner), 19, 20, 21.

Index

arms 8

bones 12
breathing 14

elbows 6, 8

faces 7
families 21
feet 4, 11
food 13

grandparents 20, 21

hair 5, 20
hands 9
health 13, 16
hospitals 19

illness 19

legs 4, 10, 11

noses 14

old age 20

parents 21
parts of the body 6

rest 17

size 4
skeletons 12
skin 5
sleep 17
sport 16

toes 11

washing 15